DINOSAUR PROFILES

ORNITHOLESTES

Titles in the Dinosaur Profiles series include:

DINOSAUR PROFILES

ORNITHOLESTES

Text by Fabio Marco Dalla Vecchia
Illustrations by Leonello Calvetti and Luca Massini

BLACKBIRCH PRESS

An imprint of Thomson Gale, a part of The Thomson Corporation

THOMSON
™
GALE

Detroit • New York • San Francisco • New Haven, Conn. • Waterville, Maine • London

Computer illustrations 3D and 2D: Leonello Calvetti and Luca Massini

Photographs: page 20–21 Lester V. Bergman/CORBIS

LIBRARY OF CONGRESS CATALOGING-IN-PUBLICATION DATA

Dalla Vecchia, Fabio Marco.
Ornitholestes / text by Fabio Marco Dalla Vecchia ; Illustrations by Leonello Calvetti and Luca Massini.
    p. cm.—(Dinosaur profiles)
Includes bibliographical references and index.
ISBN-13: 978-1-4103-0740-8 (hardcover)
ISBN-10: 1-4103-0740-9 (hardcover)
1. Ornitholestes—Juvenile literature. 2. Dinosaurs—Evolution—Juvenile literature.
I. Calvetti, Leonello, ill. II. Massini, Luca, ill. III. Title.

QE862.S3D397 2007
567.912—dc22
                                                                        2006103378

CONTENTS

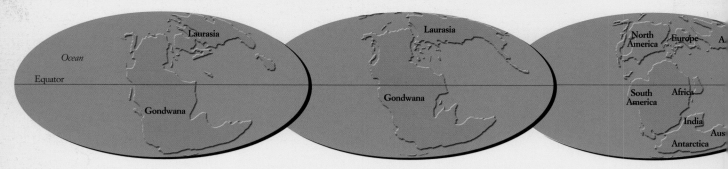

Late Triassic
228–206 million years ago

Early Jurassic
206–176 million years ago

Middle Jurassic
176–161 millions of years

A Changing World

Earth's long history began 4.6 billion years ago. Dinosaurs are some of the most fascinating animals from the planet's long past.

The word *dinosaur* comes from the word *dinosauria*. This word was invented by the English scientist Richard Owen in 1842. It comes from two Greek words, *deinos* and *sauros*. Together, these words mean "terrifying lizard."

The dinosaur era, also called the Mesozoic era, lasted from 228 million years ago to 65 million years ago. It is divided into three periods. The first, the Triassic period, lasted 42 million years. The second, the Jurassic period, lasted 61 million years. The third, the Cretaceous period, lasted 79 million years. Dinosaurs ruled the world for a huge time span of 160 million years.

Like dinosaurs, mammals appeared at the end of the Triassic period. During the time of dinosaurs, mammals were small animals the size of a mouse. Only after dinosaurs became extinct did mammals develop into the many forms that exist today. Humans never met Mesozoic dinosaurs. The dinosaurs were gone nearly 65 million years before humans appeared on Earth.

Late Jurassic
161–144 million years ago

Early Cretaceous
144–100 million years ago

Late Cretaceous
100–65 million years ago

Dinosaurs changed in time. Stegosaurus and Brachiosaurus no longer existed when Tyrannosaurus and Triceratops appeared 75 million years later.

The dinosaur world was different from today's world. The climate was warmer, with few extremes. The position of the continents was different. Plants were constantly changing, and grass did not even exist.

7

A SMALL PREDATOR

The name *Ornitholestes* comes from Greek and means "bird robber." The paleontologist Henry Fairfield Osborn gave this dinosaur its name. Osborn believed that because of its size, *Ornitholestes* would have been able to catch only small prey such as birds. But birds did not exist at the same time as Ornitholestes.

Ornitholestes was much smaller than other predators that lived where it did, such as Allosaurus and Ceratosaurus. It was no more than 6 feet (2m) long and only about 1.5 feet (0.5m) tall at the hip. It had a slight build and probably weighed between 22 and 33 pounds (10 to 15kg). It had a very long tail.

Ornitholestes lived in North America toward the end of the late Jurassic period, 155 to 148 million years ago. The remains of this dinosaur have been discovered only in what is today Wyoming.

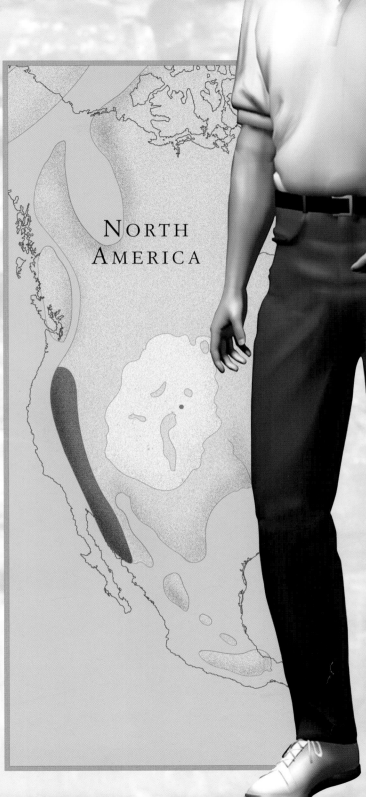

is map shows part of North America
ring the late Jurassic period. The
own areas show mountains. The red
t shows where an Ornitholestes fossil
as discovered.

NORTH
AMERICA

ORNITHOLESTES BABIES

No fossils of Ornitholestes eggs or nests
have ever been found. So scientists do not
know exactly what they looked like.
Ornitholestes may have built nests like
those of other small predators that lived
later. These nests would have been round
and open. They may have had a raised
mud rim, like the nests of some birds.

TINY MEALS

The young Ornitholestes could have caught only insects or small animals. Such food was plentiful on the plains where this dinosaur lived. Prey animals probably included lizards, frogs, salamanders, and small mammals similar to rats. Young Ornitholestes may also have eaten fish that they caught in brooks and rivers.

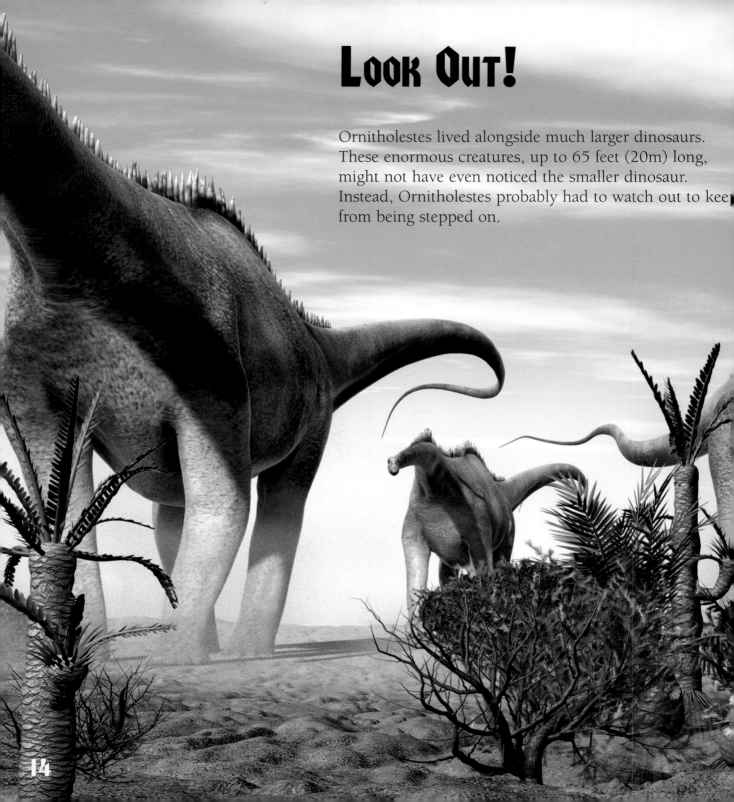

LOOK OUT!

Ornitholestes lived alongside much larger dinosaurs. These enormous creatures, up to 65 feet (20m) long, might not have even noticed the smaller dinosaur. Instead, Ornitholestes probably had to watch out to kee from being stepped on.

SMALL BUT FIERCE

Even though it was decidedly small, Ornitholestes was still a predator. An adult might well hunt a helpless, small, plant-eating dinosaur such as Othnelia, although it was probably rare in the American plains. Or the young of the larger dinosaurs might fall victim to our dinosaur if their parents were not on guard.

THE ORNITHOLESTES BODY

The Ornitholestes skull was about 5.5 inches (14cm) long. This dinosaur probably had a small crest or horn at the end of its snout. Its front teeth were cone-shaped, and the back teeth were jagged like a steak knife and curved.

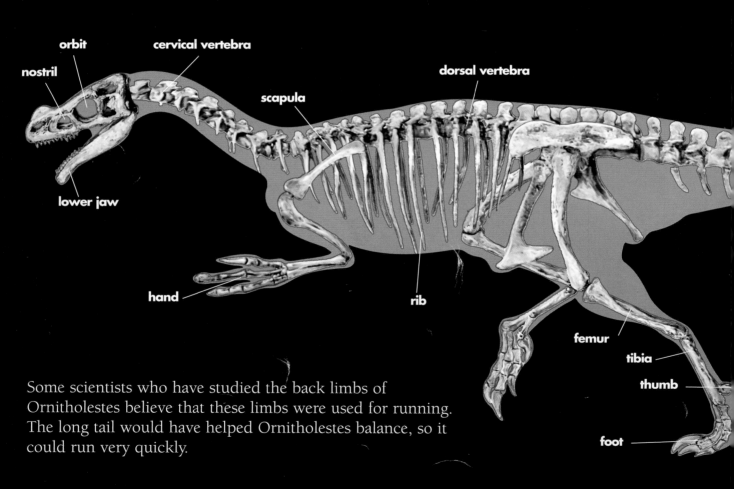

Some scientists who have studied the back limbs of Ornitholestes believe that these limbs were used for running. The long tail would have helped Ornitholestes balance, so it could run very quickly.

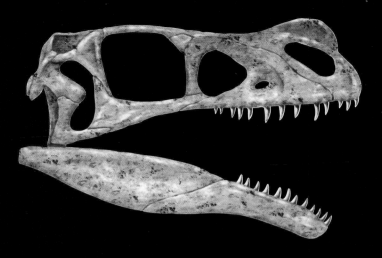

This view shows an Ornitholestes skull from the side.

caudal vertebra

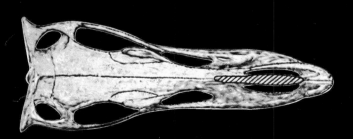

This view shows an Ornitholestes skull from above.

Digging Up Ornitholestes

Only one Ornitholestes fossil has ever been found. It was discovered in 1900 at the Bone Cabin Quarry fossil site in Wyoming. The fossil is on display at the American Museum of Natural History in New York City.

The Bone Cabin Quarry is famous because the bones of many gigantic dinosaurs have been found there. The quarry was named after a cabin built by a trapper. The cabin was made entirely out of dinosaur bones.

This is a wall of a cabin built completely of dinosaur bones. It is located in Wyoming.

The Chicxculub crater along the Yucatán Peninsula of Mexico was formed 65.5 million years ago by the impact of a meteorite. Many scientists believe that the impact caused changes in climate that led to the great extinction of dinosaurs at the end of the Mesozoic era.

- Coelurus, U.S., 155–148 million years ago

- Compsognathus, Germany and France, 150 million years ago

COELUROSAURIANS

...all, relatively primitive theropods such as Ornitholestes ...ve been found in Jurassic and Early Cretaceous rocks, ...hough they are rather rare. Recently it was discovered ...at Coelurus and Ornitholestes are closely related.

...posite: **This map shows sites where the ...elurosaurians pictured below have been found.**

● **Scipionyx, Italy, 110 million years ago**

● **Ornitholestes, U.S., 155–148 million years ago**

THE GREAT EXTINCTION

Sixty-five million years ago, around 80 million years after the time of Ornitholestes, dinosaurs became extinct. This may have happened because a large meteorite struck Earth. A wide crater caused by a meteorite 65 million years ago has been located along the coast of the Yucatán Peninsula in Mexico. The impact of the meteorite would have produced an enormous amount of dust. This dust would have stayed suspended in the atmosphere and blocked sunlight for a long time. A lack of sunlight would have caused a drastic drop in Earth's temperature and killed plants. The plant-eating dinosaurs would have died, starved and frozen. As a result, meat-eating dinosaurs would have had no prey and would also have starved.

Some scientists believe dinosaurs did not die out completely. They think that birds were feathered dinosaurs that survived the great extinction. That would make the present-day chicken and all of its feathered relatives descendants of the large dinosaurs.

THE EVOLUTION OF DINOSAURS

The oldest dinosaur fossils are 220–225 million years old and have been found mainly in South America. They have also been found in Africa, India, and North America. Dinosaurs probably evolved from small and nimble bipedal reptiles like the Triassic Lagosuchus of Argentina. Dinosaurs were able to rule the world because their legs were held directly under the body, like those of modern mammals. This made them faster and less clumsy than other reptiles.

Since 1887, dinosaurs have been divided into two groups based on the structure of their hips. Saurischian dinosaurs had hips shaped like those of modern lizards. Ornithischian dinosaurs had hips shaped like those of modern birds.

Triceratops is one of the ornithischian dinosaurs, whose hip bones (inset) are shaped like those of modern birds.

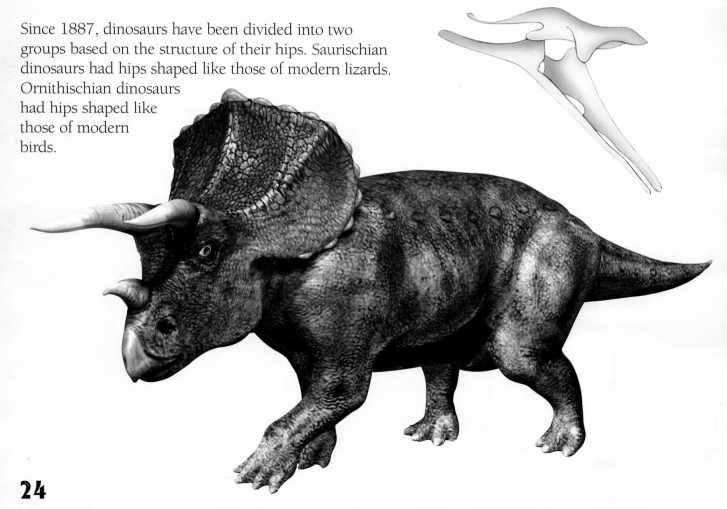

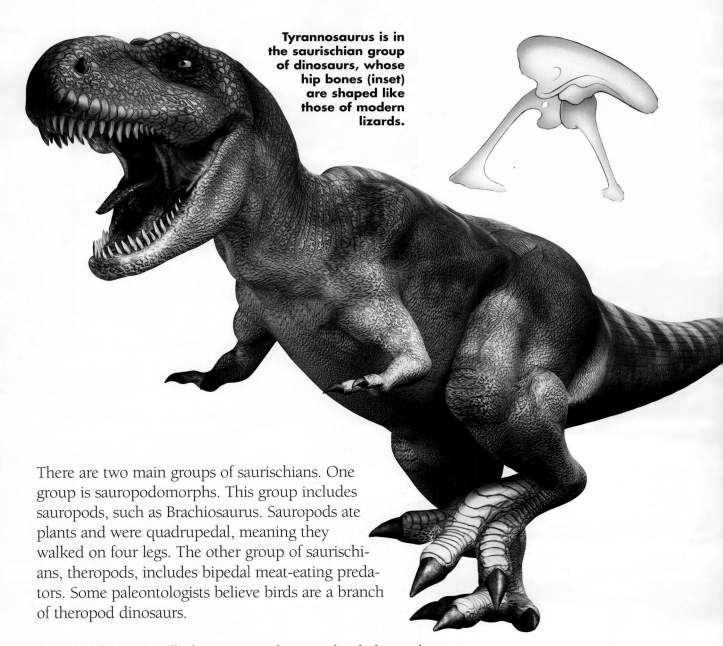

Tyrannosaurus is in the saurischian group of dinosaurs, whose hip bones (inset) are shaped like those of modern lizards.

There are two main groups of saurischians. One group is sauropodomorphs. This group includes sauropods, such as Brachiosaurus. Sauropods ate plants and were quadrupedal, meaning they walked on four legs. The other group of saurischians, theropods, includes bipedal meat-eating predators. Some paleontologists believe birds are a branch of theropod dinosaurs.

Ornithischians are all plant eaters. They are divided into three groups. Thyreophorans include the quadrupedal stegosaurians, including Stegosaurus, and ankylosaurians, including Ankylosaurus. The other two groups are ornithopods, which includes Edmontosaurus and marginocephalians.

A Dinosaur's Family Tree

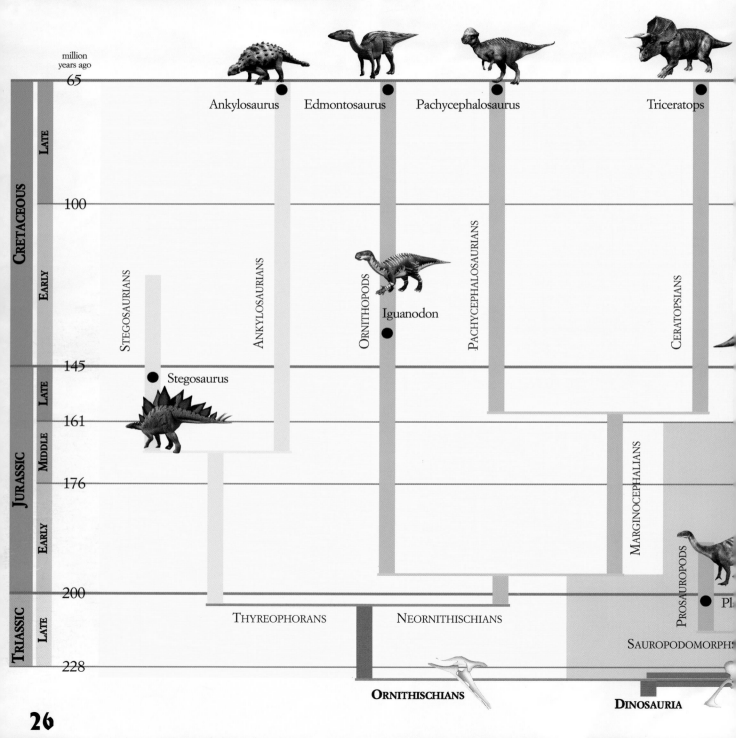

million
years ago

CRETACEOUS

JURASSIC

TRIASSIC

LATE

EARLY

LATE

MIDDLE

EARLY

LATE

65

100

145

161

176

200

228

Ankylosaurus

Edmontosaurus

Pachycephalosaurus

Triceratops

STEGOSAURIANS

Stegosaurus

ANKYLOSAURIANS

ORNITHOPODS

Iguanodon

PACHYCEPHALOSAURIANS

CERATOPSIANS

MARGINOCEPHALIANS

PROSAUROPODS

Pl

THYREOPHORANS

NEORNITHISCHIANS

SAUROPODOMORPHS

ORNITHISCHIANS

DINOSAURIA

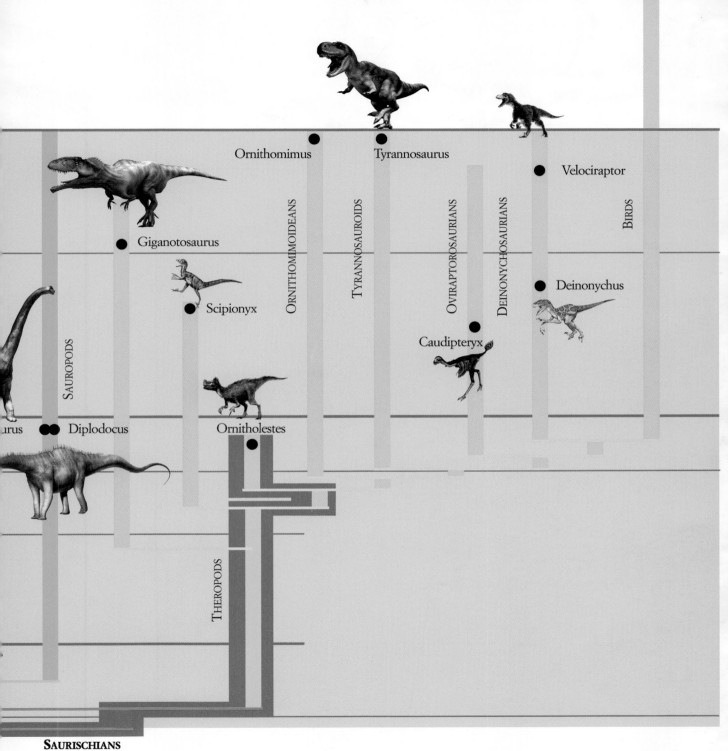

Giganotosaurus

Ornithomimus

Tyrannosaurus

Velociraptor

ORNITHOMIMOIDEANS

TYRANNOSAUROIDS

OVIRAPTOROSAURIANS

DEINONYCHOSAURIANS

BIRDS

Scipionyx

Deinonychus

Caudipteryx

SAUROPODS

...urus   Diplodocus

Ornitholestes

THEROPODS

SAURISCHIANS

27

GLOSSARY

Bipedal moving on two feet

Caudal related to the tail

Cervical related to the neck

Cretaceous period the period of geological time between 144 and 65 million years ago

Dorsal related to the back

Evolution changes in living things over time

Femur thigh bone

Fossil part of a living thing, such as a skeleton or leaf imprint, that has been preserved in Earth's crust from an earlier geological age

Jurassic period the period of geological time between 206 and 144 million years ago

Mesozoic era the period of geological time between 228 and 65 million years ago

Meteorite a piece of iron or rock that falls to Earth from space

Orbit the opening in the skull surrounding the eye.

Paleontologist a scientist who studies prehistoric life

Predator an animal that hunts other animals for food

Prey an animal that is hunted by other animals for food

Quadrupedal moving on four feet

Skeleton the structure of an animal body, made up of bones

Skull the bones that form the head and face

Tibia shinbone

Triassic period the period of geological time between 248 and 206 million years ago

Vertebra a bone of the spine

For More Information

Books

Tim Haines and Paul Chambers, *The Complete Guide to Prehistoric Life.* Richmond Hill, ON: Firefly, 2006.

Chris Maynard, *The Best Book of Dinosaurs.* Boston: Kingfisher, 2005.

Steve Parker, *Dinosaurus: The Complete Guide to Dinosaurs.* Richmond Hill, ON: Firefly, 2003.

Web Sites

Prehistoric Life
http://www.bbc.co.uk/sn/prehistoric_life/
This section of the BBC Web site contains a great deal of information about dinosaurs, including galleries of illustrations along with games and quizzes.

The Smithsonian National Museum of Natural History
http://www.nmnh.si.edu/paleo/dino/
A virtual tour of the Smithsonian's National Museum of Natural History dinosaur exhibits.

Walking with Dinosaurs
http://www.abc.net.au/dinosaurs/default.htm
The fact files section of this Web site contains information about many different dinosaurs, including Ornitholestes.

ABOUT THE AUTHOR

Fabio Marco Dalla Vecchia is the curator of the Paleontological Museum of Monfalcone in Gorizia, Italy. He has participated in several paleontological field works in Italy and other countries and has directed paleontological excavations in Italy. He is the author of more than 50 scientific articles that have been published in national and international journals.

INDEX

INDEX